Working with
Electricity and
Magnetism

BY KATHY FURGANG

TABLE OF CONTENTS

Introduction

Electricity and **magnetism** are forces that occur in nature. They are two of the most useful forces on Earth.

Have you ever noticed that clothes stick together after they come out of a clothes dryer? Did you ever get a shock from touching someone or something on a dry winter day? If so, you have observed **static electricity**.

There is another kind of electricity you can observe. **Current electricity** makes computers, video games, telephones, and the lights in your home and school work.

Current electricity provides power for stadium lights.

Electromagnets can lift heavy metal objects.

Magnetism affects your life in many ways, too. Magnets have uses far beyond that of holding papers on a refrigerator. They are used in tools such as can openers and screwdrivers. They keep refrigerator and cabinet doors closed. A kind of magnet called an **electromagnet** can be used to lift cars and other heavy pieces of metal.

In this book, you will learn about these forces—static electricity, current electricity, magnetism, and electromagnetism. You will experiment with each force and discover the fun of working with electricity and magnetism.

Static Electricity

On a dry winter day, you pull a wool hat off your head and discover that your hair is standing on end. What makes this happen? The answer is static electricity!

To understand what static electricity is, you must know something about the tiny particles that make up everything around you. These tiny particles are called **atoms**.

Atoms are made up of even smaller particles. Two of these particles are found in the nucleus, or center, of the atom. They are called protons and neutrons. Traveling around the nucleus are particles called **electrons**.

Protons and electrons have a property called charge. Protons have a positive charge (+). Electrons have a negative charge (−). Neutrons have no charge.

Protons and neutrons are found in the nucleus, or center, of an atom. Electrons circle the nucleus.

NEON ATOM

nucleus containing protons and neutrons

electrons outside the nucleus

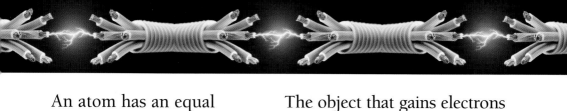

An atom has an equal number of protons (+) and electrons (–). This makes an atom electrically neutral. Because all objects are made up of electrically neutral atoms, all objects are electrically neutral.

When certain objects are rubbed together, however, electrons from one object can be transferred to the other object. This means that one object gains electrons and the other object loses electrons.

The object that gains electrons has a negative charge. The object that loses electrons has a positive charge. This is what happens when a wool hat rubs against your hair.

The electrons that are transferred from one object to the other do not move any farther. They build up on the object. This buildup is called static electricity.

Rubbing separates charges, giving one object a positive charge and the other object a negative charge. This person is touching a device that produces static electricity. The charge that has built up is large enough to make her hair stand on end!

OPPOSITES ATTRACT

Have you ever heard the phrase "opposites attract"? Not only is it true, it's a law of nature! This law applies to electrical charges. Positive and negative charges, or opposite charges, attract each other. Like charges repel, or move away from, each other.

Objects do not have to touch in order to attract or repel each other. An invisible electric field surrounds electrically charged objects. The activity on the facing page will demonstrate the law of charges as you bend a stream of water.

According to the law of charges, like charges repel and opposite charges attract. The cat is experiencing this law. The balloon has been given a negative charge. It attracts the positive charges in the cat's fur.

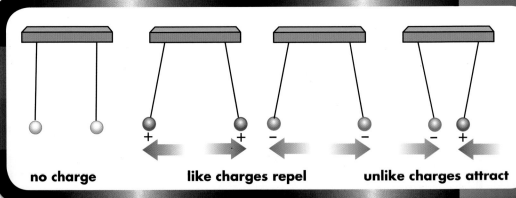

no charge   like charges repel   unlike charges attract

BENDING WATER

What you need

- plastic pen
- wool fabric
- faucet

What to do

1. Turn the faucet on to make a slow, smooth, even flow of water about as thick as a soda straw.

2. Hold the plastic pen about an inch away from the stream of water. Do not get the pen wet. Does anything happen to the stream of water? Record what you see.

3. Now rub the pen with the piece of wool fabric at least 10 times. This will transfer electrons from the wool to the pen. The pen will then have a negative charge.

4. Hold the pen about an inch away from the running water. Slowly move the pen closer to the stream of water. Do not get the pen wet. Does anything happen to the stream of water? Record what you see.

ENERGY ON THE MOVE

Rub your shoes across a carpet and then touch a metal doorknob. Zap! You get an electric shock. Why?

You read on page 5 that static electricity is the buildup of electrons on an object. These extra electrons do not stay on the object forever. They eventually leave the object. Sometimes they move to another object. More often they escape into the air. This movement of extra electrons is called an electric discharge.

As a result of an electric discharge, the charged object loses its static electricity. It becomes neutral again.

Rubbing your shoes across the carpet transfers electrons from the carpet to you. When the extra electrons discharge to the doorknob, you feel an electric shock. You might also see a spark or hear a crackle of noise.

An electric discharge can be slow and quiet or fast and noisy. Often it is accompanied by a shock or spark of light.

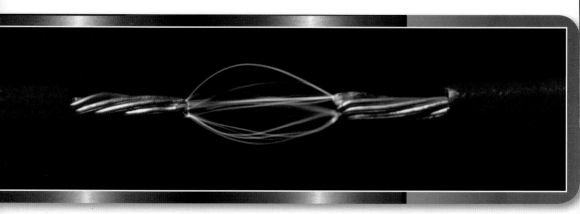

The discharge of static electricity from one metal object to another can be seen as a spark.

Point

Make Connections

Think about a time when lightning surprised or scared you. Tell a group member about your experience.

One of the most dramatic discharges of static electricity is lightning. During a storm, water droplets and ice particles in clouds are tossed around by winds. This movement causes charges to be transferred. Some parts of the clouds become positively charged. Other parts become negatively charged.

When the charges discharge, lightning can occur between clouds and the ground or between clouds themselves. Sometimes lightning occurs within a cloud itself.

Certain materials allow electric charges to move through them easily. These materials are called **conductors**.

Lightning is a very dramatic discharge of static electricity.

Most metals are good conductors. Earth is a good conductor, as is water.

Materials such as glass and plastic do not allow electric charges to move through them easily. Such materials are called **insulators**.

Conductors	Insulators
metals	glass
heated gases	rubber
water	plastic
human body	wood

STATIC PICKUP GAME

What you need

- cotton or wool fabric
- plastic comb
- tissue paper
- newspaper
- plastic wrap
- aluminum foil
- salt
- pepper
- wooden ruler
  or toothbrush

What to do

1. Cut the newspaper, tissue paper, plastic wrap, and aluminum foil into small pieces. Keep the pieces of each material in their own pile. Make a small pile of salt and another of pepper.

2. Make a chart similar to the one shown below.

3. Charge the comb by rubbing it several times with the cotton fabric.

Materials	Results
tissue paper	???
newspaper	???
plastic wrap	???
aluminum foil	???
salt	???
pepper	???

4. Move the charged comb close to the pile of tissue-paper pieces. Record what happens.

5. Rub the comb with the fabric to charge it again. Repeat step 4 with the pieces of newspaper. Record what happens.

6. Repeat step 4 for each of the remaining materials and record the results. Which materials could be picked up with the charged comb?

7. Try the activity again. This time use a wooden ruler or the end of a plastic toothbrush instead of a comb. Add a column to your chart to record the results.

It's a FACT

Most photocopy machines use static electricity in their operation. Inside the copier there is a cylinder called a drum. The copier gives the drum a positive charge.

Light shines on the paper you want to copy. It's reflected from white areas but not from dark areas.

When reflected light hits the drum, it changes the positive charge to a negative charge at that spot. As a result, the drum has an image of the paper you want to copy "painted" in positive and negative charges.

The copier puts a negative charge on powdered ink and shakes it onto the turning drum. The ink sticks to the parts of the drum that have a positive charge. The ink is repelled by the parts of the drum that have a negative charge.

The copier puts a positive charge on a clean sheet of paper. The paper draws the powdered ink onto it. The ink is fused to the paper by heat.

Current Electricity

We rely on current electricity every day. It makes radios, televisions, lights, appliances, clocks, and tools work.

Current electricity is the flow of electrons through a wire or other conductor. Remember, a conductor is a material that allows electrons to move through it easily.

All current electricity moves through a **circuit**. A circuit is a closed path. An electric circuit always consists of a source of electricity, conducting wires, and a device that uses the electricity. A circuit often has a switch, too.

Suppose you want to make a lightbulb work. You will need a lightbulb and a source of electricity, such as a **battery**. You will also need a conductor, such as copper wire, and a switch.

The electricity flows from the negative part of the battery through the circuit to the positive part of the battery. As it flows through the delicate wire inside the lightbulb, it produces heat. The heated wire gives off light.

Batteries come in a variety of shapes, sizes, and voltages.

The switch in a circuit opens and closes the circuit. Electric current can flow only when a circuit is closed. When the switch is on, the circuit is complete, or closed. Electricity flows. The light lights. When the switch is off, the circuit is broken. It is incomplete, or open. Electricity cannot flow. The light does not light.

No electricity can flow through an open circuit. When the switch is flipped, the circuit is closed. Electricity can flow.

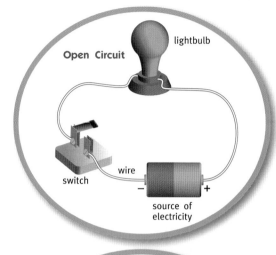

Open Circuit

lightbulb

wire

switch

source of electricity

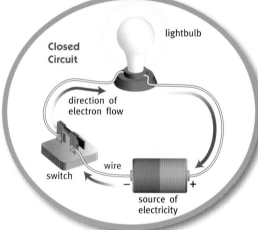

Closed Circuit

lightbulb

direction of electron flow

wire

switch

source of electricity

It's a FACT

In 1879, inventor and scientist Thomas Alva Edison demonstrated a very important invention—the lightbulb. The bulb he invented glowed hot and gave off light when electricity flowed through it. His invention is still in use today. Imagine what life would be like without the lightbulb!

COMPLETE A CIRCUIT

What you need

- 12 inches of insulated copper wire
- D-cell battery
- flashlight bulb
- tape
- paper clip
- thumbtack
- cardboard
- wire cutters

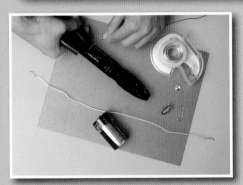

What to do

1. Cut the copper wire into two 6-inch pieces.

2. Have an adult cut 1 inch of the insulation off each end of the pieces of wire. This will expose the ends of the wire.

3. Tape one end of a piece of wire to the end of the battery marked with a negative (–) symbol.

4. Wrap the other end of the wire around the metal end of the flashlight bulb. Tape it in place, being careful not to cover the bottom tip of the bulb.

5. Place the exposed part of the bottom of the flashlight bulb on the cardboard so the bulb stands up. Tape the wire down so that the bulb does not move.

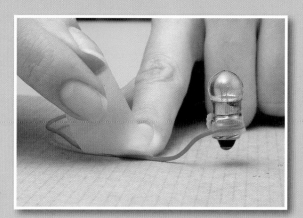

6. Tape one end of the other piece of wire to the end of the battery marked with a positive (+) symbol.

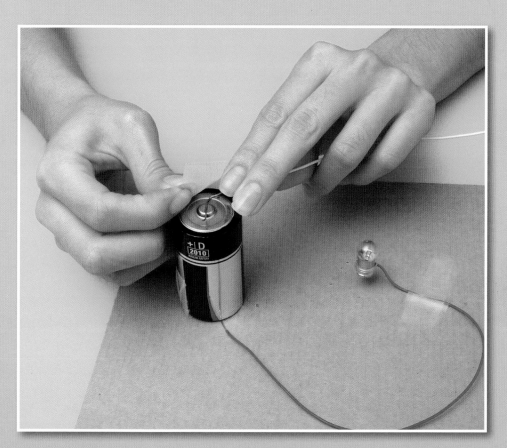

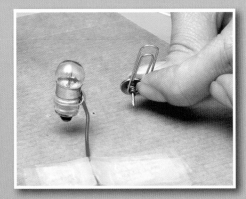

7. Wrap the other end of the wire around the thumbtack. Push the end of the thumbtack through the end of the paper clip and into the piece of cardboard. You should be able to rotate the paper clip once it is tacked into the cardboard.

8. The tack should be placed close enough to the flashlight bulb so that the paper clip can touch the bottom of the bulb. The thumbtack will hold down both the wire and the paper clip. This will be your switch.

9. Rotate the paper-clip switch so that it touches the bottom of the bulb. You closed the circuit. The bulb goes on.

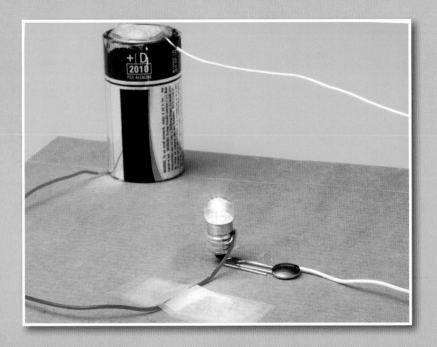

10. Rotate the paper-clip switch again so that the circuit is open. The bulb goes off.

11. Experiment to find a way to make the bulb light without using the paper clip. How else can you close the circuit containing the battery, wire, and bulb?

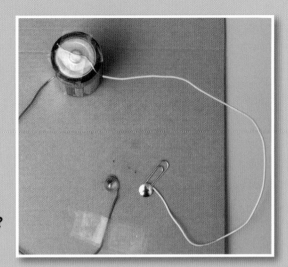

It's a FACT

Electrical devices can produce too much heat. Circuits can be overloaded with too many appliances. Such situations can cause a fire. A fuse or circuit breaker can protect a home. When too many appliances are loaded on a circuit, the fuse blows or the circuit breaker switches off, stopping the flow of electricity.

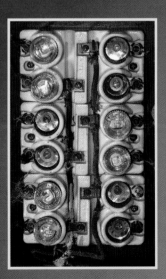

circuit-breaker box   fuse box

Magnetism

Did you know that magnets have been used for more than 2,000 years? In ancient Greece, people living in an area called Magnesia discovered an unusual rock. The rock attracted iron or objects containing iron. As if by magic, the rock stuck to these objects! The rock the Greeks discovered is called magnetite. Magnetite was the first magnet.

In ancient China, travelers used a similar rock to guide them on long trips. The rock always pointed in the same direction when it was hung from a string. The direction it pointed in was toward a northern star called the leading star, or lodestar. The rock was named lodestone, which means "leading stone." It worked much like today's magnetic compass.

Today, magnets are used in many ways. Compasses, can openers, refrigerator doors, doorbells, telephones, audiotapes, and videotapes are just some of the things that use magnets and magnetism.

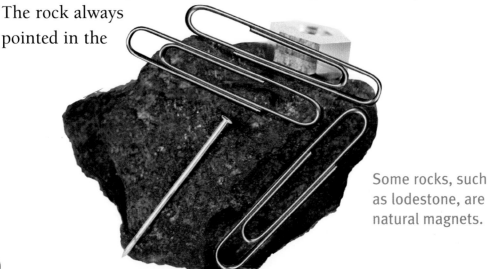

Some rocks, such as lodestone, are natural magnets.

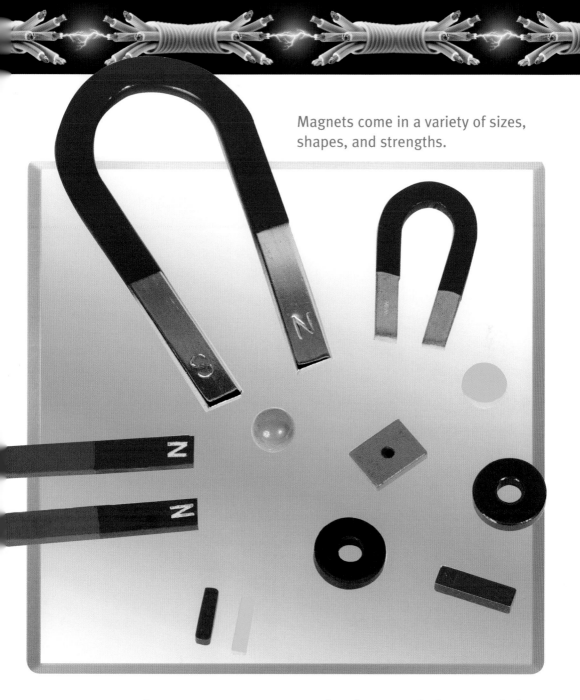

Magnets come in a variety of sizes, shapes, and strengths.

Magnets today come in a variety of sizes and shapes. These shapes include bar magnets, horseshoe magnets, and disc magnets.

Many modern magnets are made of iron, cobalt, or nickel, which are all metals. Others are made of a material called alnico. It is a combination of aluminum, nickel, cobalt, and iron.

WORKING WITH MAGNETS

How do magnets work? Magnetism is a force. It can attract or repel. The area around a magnet in which magnetic forces attract or repel is called a **magnetic field**. This invisible field spreads out in an arc from the ends of a magnet.

The ends of a magnet are called the magnet's **poles**. Every magnet has a north pole and a south pole. Like positive and negative electric charges, the poles of a magnet attract or repel each other.

Unlike poles attract. The north and south poles attract each other. Like poles repel. Two north poles repel each other. Two south poles also repel each other.

Try holding two bar magnets close to each other. If the two ends attract, they are unlike, or opposite, poles. How could you tell if the ends were like poles?

It's a FACT

A magnet will work best if it is cared for properly. Try not to drop magnets. This can make them weaker. Horseshoe magnets are often stored with an iron bar across their poles. Two bar magnets of the same size should be stored stuck to each other. This keeps the magnets strong.

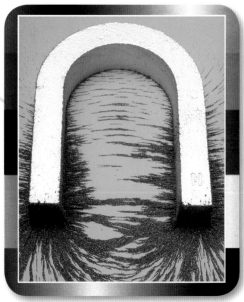

When these iron filings were scattered over the magnet, they were attracted by the magnet's magnetic field.

TEST A MAGNET'S STRENGTH

What you need
- magnets of various sizes
- paper clip • Styrofoam™ cup
- paper cup • water
- plastic cup

What to do

1. Place a paper clip in an empty Styrofoam™ cup. Use the different magnets to attract the clip through the cup. Do not put the magnet in the cup. Use it only from the outside of the cup. Which magnets are strong enough to do this?

2. Try the activity again with water in the cup. Can you lift the paper clip through the cup and the water?

3. Repeat steps 1 and 2 using a paper cup.

4. Identify the strongest magnet you have. Use it to try steps 1 and 2 again with a thin plastic cup instead of a paper cup.

IT'S A MAGNETIC WORLD

If you hang a bar magnet from a string and let it stop swinging, the magnet's ends will face north and south. That's because Earth itself is surrounded by a magnetic field. The north and south ends of magnets were named for the poles of Earth that they point to.

Many hikers, sailors, and pilots rely on compasses to show them direction. A compass has a magnetized needle that points north.

You can magnetize a nail temporarily by stroking it many times with a magnet. You must move the magnet in the same direction each time. You must also lift the magnet away from the nail between strokes. The nail can now be used to pick up pins or paper clips!

✔ Point

Read More About It

Some birds, insects, fish, and other animals have tiny bits of magnetic metal in their bodies. Scientists think that these bits of metal help them find their way when they travel great distances. Using reference materials, read more about this idea.

A compass has a magnetized needle that points north.

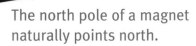

The north pole of a magnet naturally points north.

MAKE A MAGNETIC COMPASS

What you need

- bar magnet
- nail
- bowl of water
- cork
- large piece of paper
- tape
- marker

What to do

1. Fill the bowl with water. Place the bowl on a large piece of paper.

2. Float the cork in the water.

3. Stroke the nail with the bar magnet several times in the same direction. This should magnetize the nail.

4. Lay the nail on the cork. You may need to tape the nail in place. Wait for the cork to stop moving in the water.

5. Make a line or other mark on the paper to show where each end of the nail is pointing.

6. Tap the cork with your finger to make it spin.

7. Does the nail point in the same direction when it stops moving?

A MAGNETIC CAR RACE

What you need

- magnets
- metal toy cars
- paper clips
- poster board
- books
- crafts materials
- tape

What to do

1. Find two cars that roll easily.
2. Find magnets that are strong enough to attract the cars through the poster board.
3. Draw two roads on the poster board. Each road should be wide enough for a toy car. The roads should not cross. Mark each road with a "start" and "finish" line.
4. Draw scenery around the roads as you wish.

5. Place the ends of the poster board on stacks of books so that it makes a bridge. You should have enough room to move your hand under the poster board. Tape the ends in place.

6. Place a toy car on the starting line of each road.

7. Work with a partner to race the cars. Control them by moving magnets underneath the poster board. The magnets will attract the cars through the poster board.

8. Run several race trials. In each trial, use different magnets and different cars. Why do some combinations of cars and magnets work better than others?

Electromagnetism

In 1821, scientist Hans Christian Oersted was demonstrating to friends how electricity flows through a copper wire. During the experiment, he observed that the flow of current made a nearby compass needle move. He realized that there was a connection between electricity and magnetism. The discovery that an electric current is surrounded by a magnetic field led to the electromagnet.

An electromagnet is a piece of iron with a coil of wire wrapped around it. It works as a magnet only when electricity is passing through the wire. A switch turns the electromagnet on and off. Wrapping more coils of wire around the iron will make the magnet stronger.

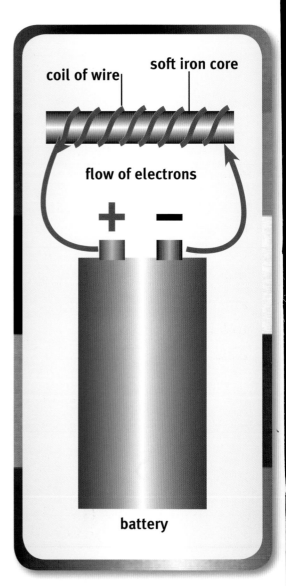

coil of wire

soft iron core

flow of electrons

+ −

battery

An electromagnet is produced by wrapping a coil of wire around a piece of soft iron. The strength of the electromagnet depends on the number of coils wrapped around it.

One of the first uses of electromagnetism was in telegraphs. In the late 1800s, telegraphs were an important method of communication. By closing a circuit for short or long periods of time, short or long bits of electric current were sent over a wire. At the other end of the wire, an electromagnet pulled a strip of metal to make it click in dots and dashes. These dots and dashes corresponded to letters and numbers established by Morse code.

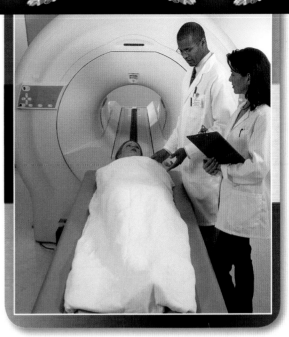

The medical technique known as MRI uses a device such as this to "see" inside the human body. Doctors use the images produced to help diagnose diseases.

This is a photograph of Samuel Morse's first telegraph. It was used to send the first telegraph message from Washington, D.C. to Baltimore, Maryland, on May 24, 1844.

Today, many junkyards use electromagnets to lift heavy objects, such as machinery and cars. Electromagnets also sort metals and other materials in recycling centers.

Electromagnets are also used in medical technology. A technique called Magnetic Resonance Imaging (MRI) uses magnetism to show a detailed view of the inside of the human body.

MAKE AN ELECTROMAGNET

What you need
- dry-cell battery
- covered copper wire
- nail
- paper clips
- tape
- scissors
- bar magnet
- wire cutters

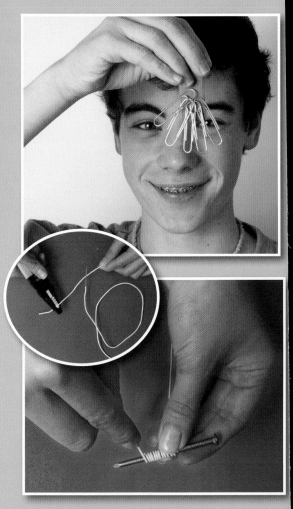

What to do

1. Use an ordinary bar magnet to pick up paper clips. How many can you lift?

2. Cut a 3-foot length of copper wire.

3. Ask an adult to cut 1 inch of the insulation off each end of the wire.

4. Wrap the wire tightly around the nail. Do not let the exposed ends touch each other.

5. Tape one end of the exposed wire to the positive end of the dry-cell battery. It will be marked with a positive (+) symbol.

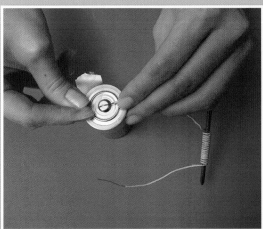

6. Touch the nail to the paper clips. Does it pick up anything? Explain.

7. Tape the other end of the exposed wire to the negative end of the dry-cell battery. It will be marked with a negative (–) symbol.

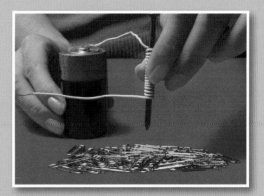

8. Touch the nail to the paper clips. Does it pick up anything? How many paper clips can it lift? Can the electromagnet lift more paper clips than the ordinary magnet?

9. You can adjust the strength of your electromagnet. First, undo a few of the coils. Can the electromagnet lift more or fewer clips now? Now add more coils. Can the electromagnet lift more or fewer clips now?

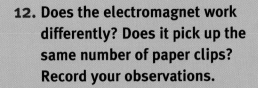

10. Remove the wire from the positive and negative ends of the battery.

11. Change the direction of the current. Take the wire that was attached to the positive end (+) of the battery and tape it to the negative end (–). Take the wire that was attached to the negative end (–) of the battery and tape it to the positive end (+).

12. Does the electromagnet work differently? Does it pick up the same number of paper clips? Record your observations.

Reread

Skim Chapters 1–4.
In which chapter did you learn the most?

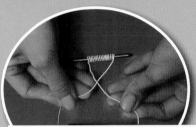

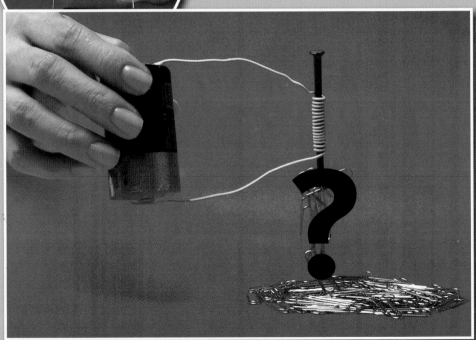

Glossary

atom   (A-tum) a tiny particle that makes up all objects (page 4)

battery   (BA-tuh-ree) a device that converts chemical energy to electrical energy (page 12)

circuit   (SER-kit) a path through which electricity moves (page 12)

conductor   (kun-DUK-ter) a material that allows electricity to flow (page 9)

current electricity   (KER-ent ih-lek-TRIH-sih-tee) the flow of electrons through a circuit or path (page 2)

electricity   (ih-lek-TRIH-sih-tee) the movement of electrons along a path (page 2)

electromagnet   (ih-lek-troh-MAG-net) a magnet powered by an electric current (page 3)

electron   (ih-LEK-trahn) a negative particle in an atom that travels around the nucleus (page 4)

insulator   (IN-suh-lay-ter) a material that stops or slows the flow of electricity (page 9)

magnetic field   (mag-NEH-tik FEELD) an area of force around a magnet or magnetized object (page 20)

magnetism   (MAG-neh-tih-zum) attracting and repelling property of magnets (page 2)

pole   (POLE) a magnetized end of a magnet (page 20)

static electricity   (STA-tik ih-lek-TRIH-sih-tee) the buildup of electrical charges (page 2)

Index

Title 1-Unsworth School